W9-AUF-646

016 GREATEST
POP & MOVIE HITS

ARRANGED BY
DAN COATES

CONTENTS

Alfred

Produced by
Alfred Music
P.O. Box 10003
Van Nuys, CA 91410-0003
alfred.com

ISBN-10: 1-4706-3347-7
ISBN-13: 978-1-4706-3347-9

Skyscrapers: © iStockphoto.com / gyn9038

ALL I ASK

Words and Music by Chri
Bruno Mars, Adele Adkins and Philip L
Arr. Dan

BRIGHT

Words and Music by Graham Sierota, Jamie Sierota,
Noah Sierota, Sydney Sierota, Jeffery Sierota and Maureen McDonald
Arr. Dan Coates

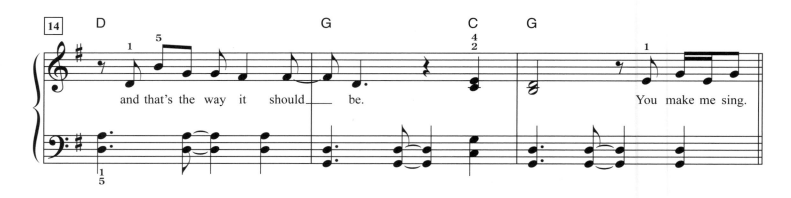

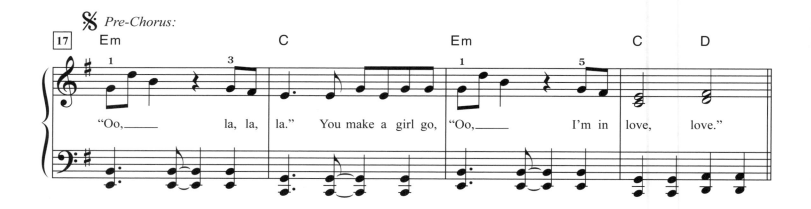

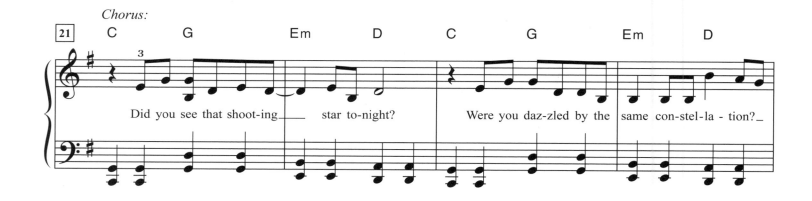

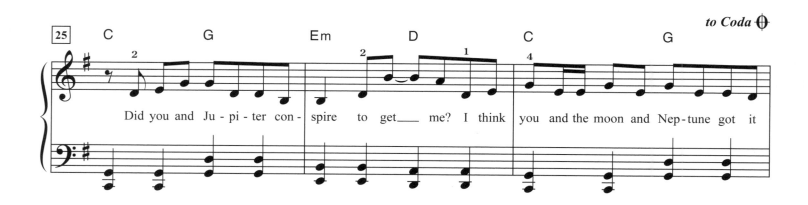

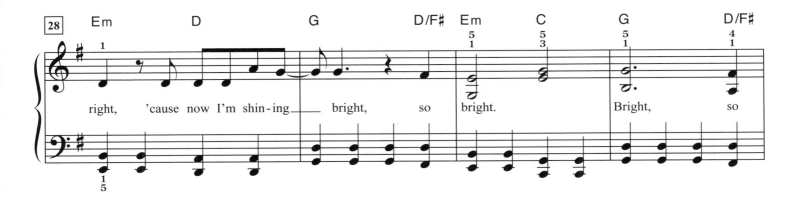

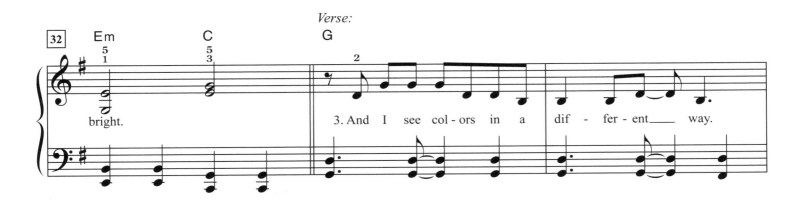

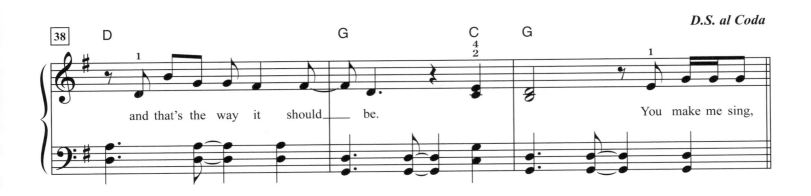

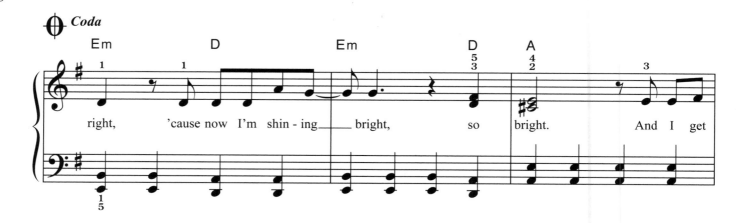

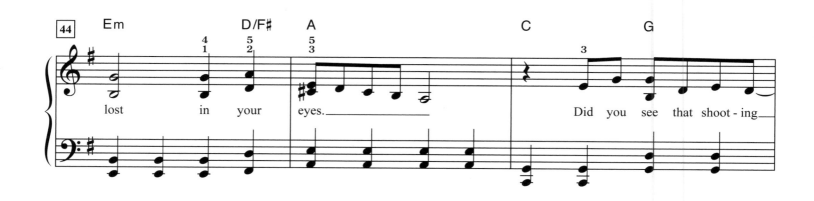

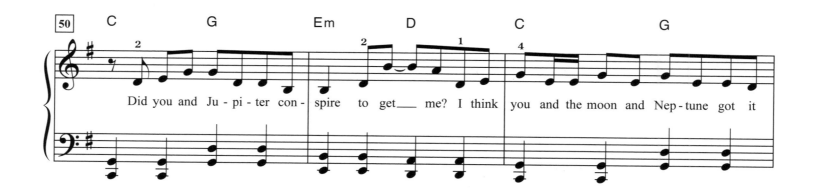

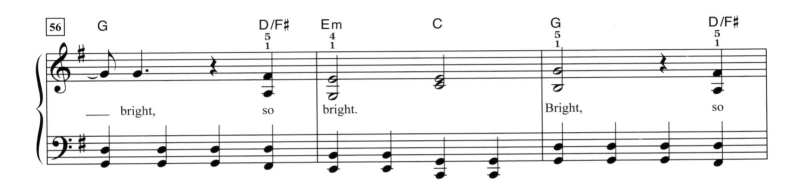

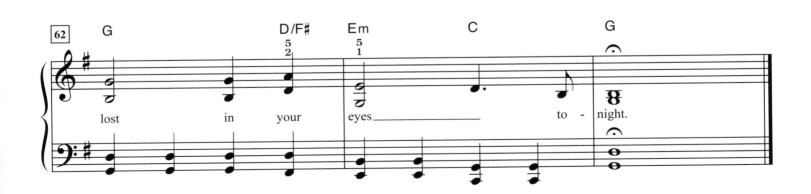

BUNDLE OF JOY

(from *Inside Out*)

Words and Music by Michael Giacchino
Arr. Dan Coates

CAN'T FEEL MY FACE

Words and Music by Ali Payami, Savan Kotecha,
Max Martin, Abel Tesfaye and Peter Svensson
Arr. Dan Coates

Pre-Chorus:

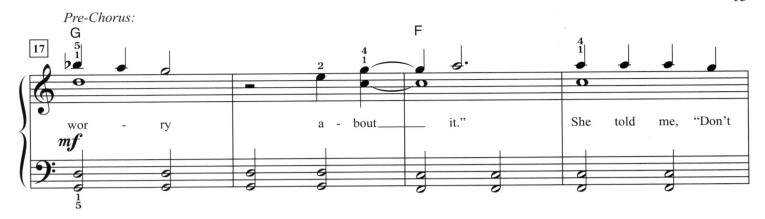

wor - ry   a - bout___ it."   She told me, "Don't

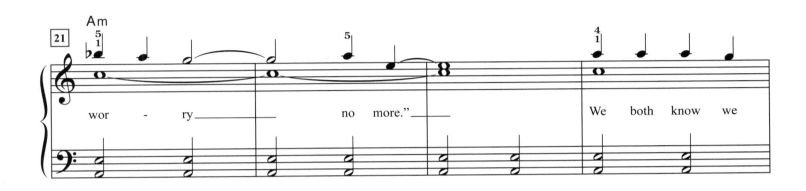

wor - ry___   no more."___   We both know we

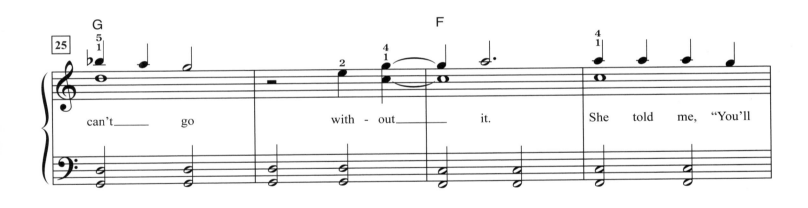

can't___ go   with - out___ it.   She told me, "You'll

nev - er   be in love."   Oh,   oh,   ooh.

14

CENTURIES

Words and Music by Suzanne Vega, Justin Tranter,
Raja Kumari, Jonathan Rotem, Michael Fonesca,
Andrew Hurley, Patrick Stumph, Pete Wentz and Joseph Trohman
Arr. Dan Coates

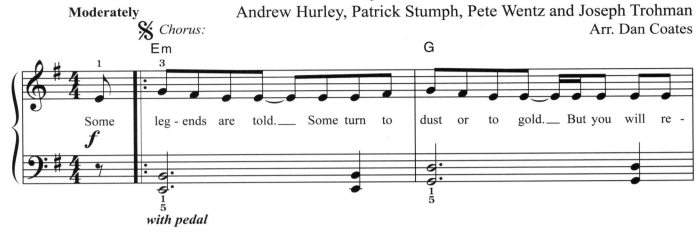

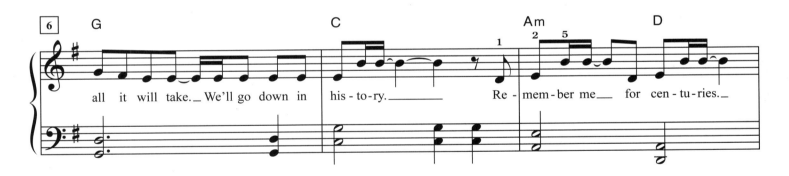

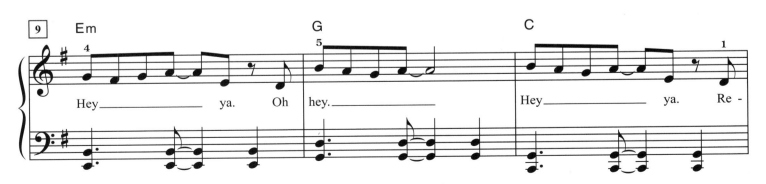

18

CHEERLEADER

Words and Music by Mark Bradford, Ryan Dillon,
Sly Dunbar, Omar Pasley and Clifton Dillon
Arr. Dan Coates

25

COOL FOR THE SUMMER

Words and Music by
Ali Payami, Savan Kotecha, Max Martin,
Alexander Kronlund and Demitria Lovato
Arr. Dan Coates

Moderately
Verse:

1. Tell me what you want, what you like. It's o - kay.
2. Tell me if I won, what if I did, what's my prize?

I'm a lit - tle cu - ri - ous too.
I just wan - na play with you too.

Tell me if it's wrong, if it's right; I don't care.
E - ven if they judge, if screw it all; do the time.

I can keep a se - cret. Could you?
I just wan - na have some fun with you. Got my

FOCUS

Words and Music by Ilya, Savan Kotecha,
Peter Svensson and Ariana Grande
Arr. Dan Coates

Moderately bright

Verse 2:
I can tell you're curious
It's written on your lips.
Ain't no need to hold it back,
Go 'head and talk your talk.
I know you're hoping that I'll react,
I know you're hoping I'm looking back.
But if my real ain't real enough
Then I don't know what is.
(To Pre-Chorus:)

GHOST TOWN

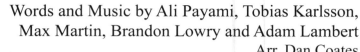

Words and Music by Ali Payami, Tobias Karlsson,
Max Martin, Brandon Lowry and Adam Lambert
Arr. Dan Coates

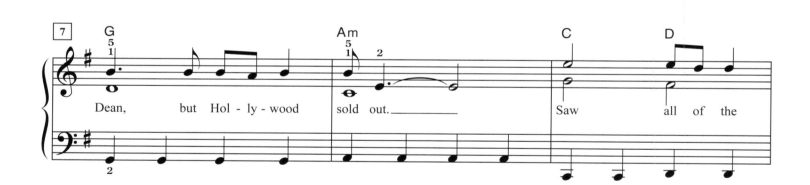

GOOD FOR YOU

Words and Music by Justin Tranter, Nick Monson,
Nolan Lambroza, Julia Michaels and Selena Gomez
Arr. Dan Coates

41

HEARTBEAT SONG

Words and Music by Audra Mae, Kelly Clarkson,
Kara Dioguardi and Jason Evigan
Arr. Dan Coates

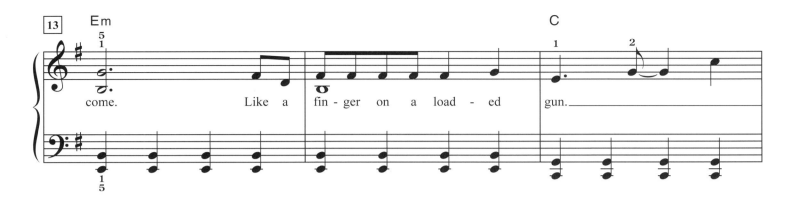

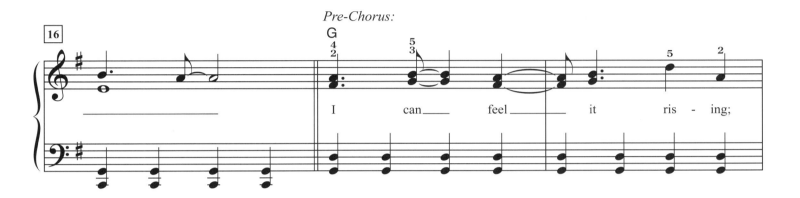

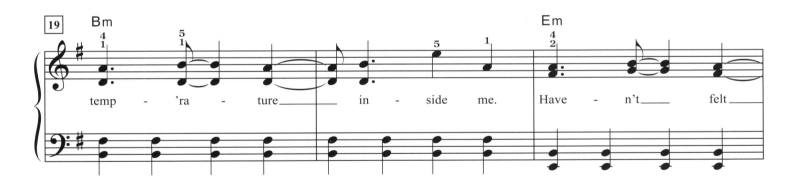

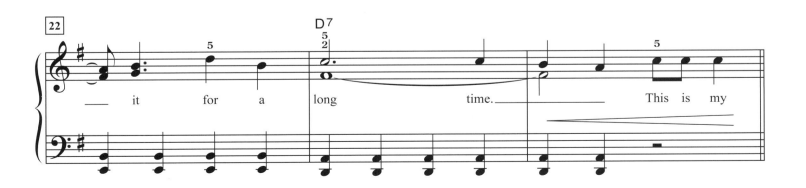

Verse 2:
I, I wasn't even gonna go out
But I never would have had a doubt,
If I'd-a known where I'd be now.
Your hands on my hips,
And my kiss on your lips.
Oh, I could do this for a long time.
(To Chorus:)

LOVE ME LIKE YOU DO

(from *Fifty Shades of Grey*)

Words and Music by Ali Payami, Ilya,
Tove Lo, Max Martin and Savan Kotecha
Arr. Dan Coates

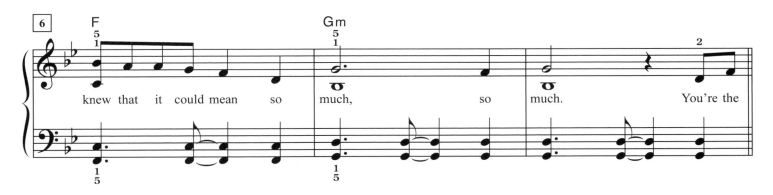

LIKE I'M GONNA LOSE YOU

Words and Music by Justin Weaver,
Caitlyn Smith and Meghan Trainor
Arr. Dan Coates

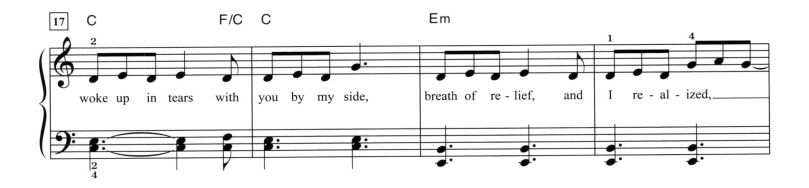

woke up in tears with you by my side, breath of re - lief, and I re - al - ized,____

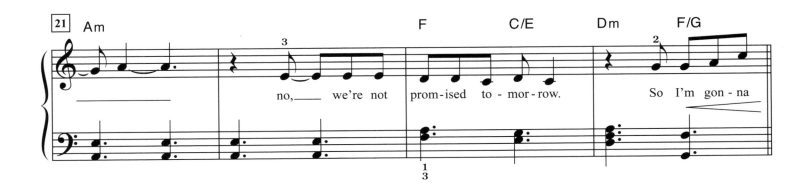

____ no,____ we're not prom - ised to - mor - row. So I'm gon - na

Chorus:

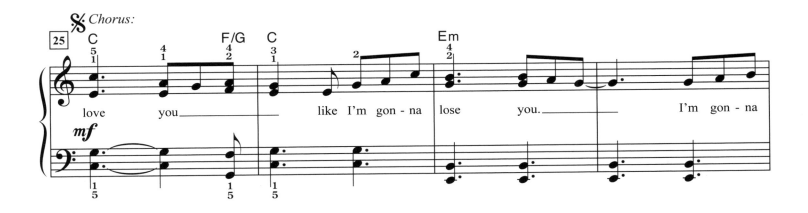

love you____ like I'm gon - na lose you.____ I'm gon - na

hold you like I'm say - ing good - bye.____ Wher - ev - er we're

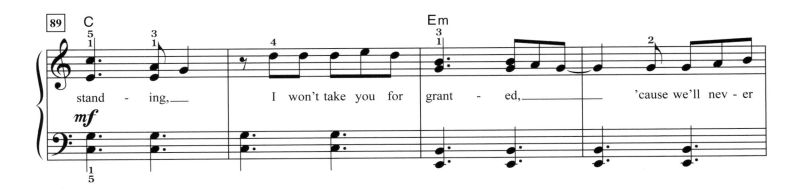

standing,___ I won't take you for grant - ed,___ 'cause we'll nev - er

know___ when,___ when we'll run out of time.___ So I'm gon - na

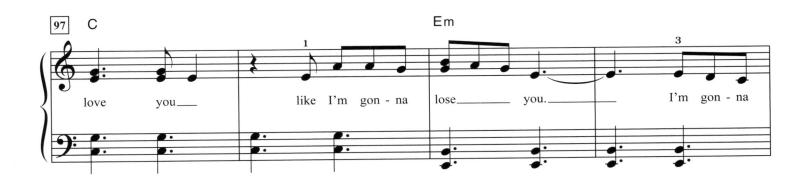

love you___ like I'm gon - na lose___ you.___ I'm gon - na

love___ you___ like I'm gon - na lose___ you.___

MARVIN GAYE

Words and Music by Jacob Luttrell,
Nick Seeley, Charlie Puth and Julie Frost
Arr. Dan Coates

ME AND MY BROKEN HEART

Words and Music by Wayne Hector, Steve Mac,
Benjamin Levin, Ammar Malik and Rob Thomas
Arr. Dan Coates

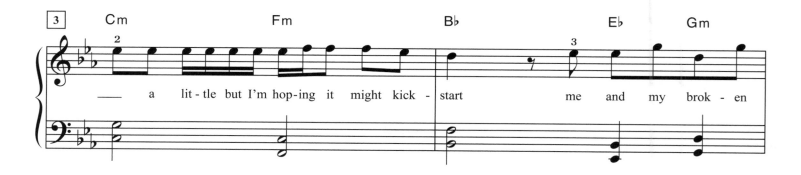

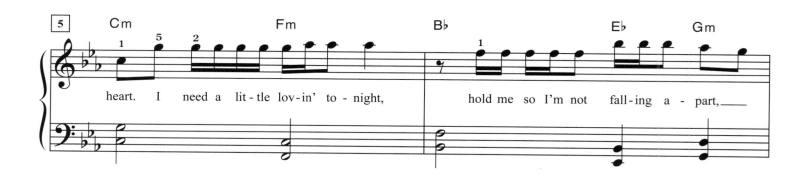

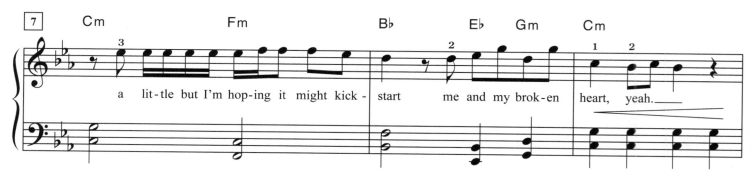

ON MY MIND

Words and Music by Ilya, Savan Kotecha,
Max Martin and Ellie Goulding
Arr. Dan Coates

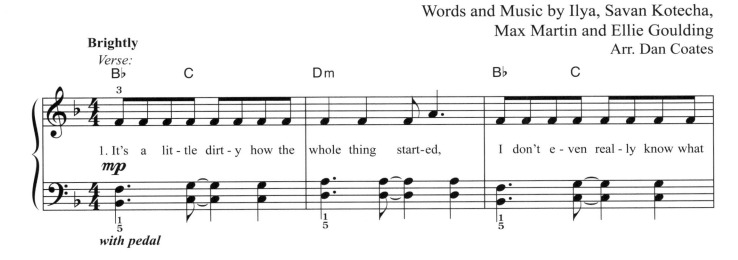

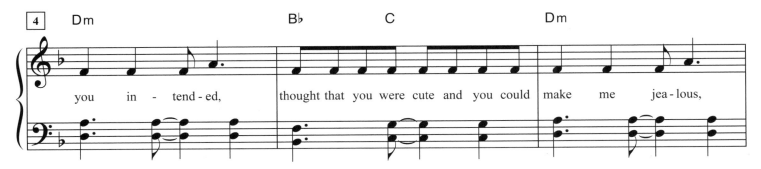

ONE CALL AWAY

Words and Music by Matthew Prime,
Justin Franks, Charlie Puth, Breyan Isaac,
Maureen McDonald and Shy Carter
Arr. Dan Coates

SHUT UP AND DANCE

Words and Music by
Ryan McMahon, Benjamin Berger, Nicholas Petricca,
Sean Waugaman, Kevin Ray and Eli Maiman
Arr. Dan Coates

SORRY

Words and Music by
Justin Tranter, Julia Michaels, Justin Bieber,
Sonny Moore and Michael Tucker
Arr. Dan Coates

Upbeat pop

Verse:

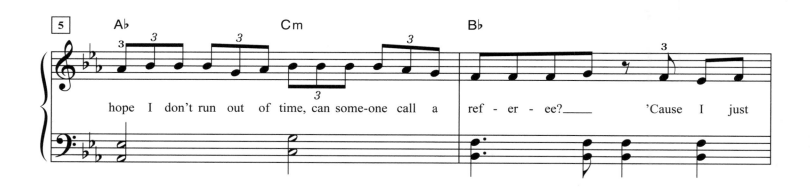

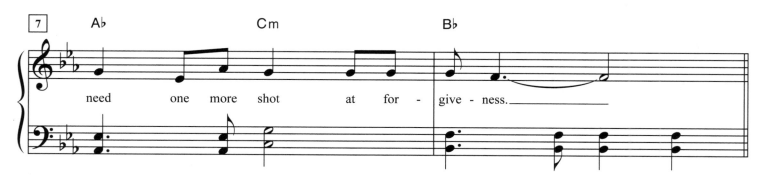

STAR WARS (MAIN THEME)

(from *Star Wars: The Force Awakens*)

Music by **JOHN WILLIAMS**
Arr. Dan Coates

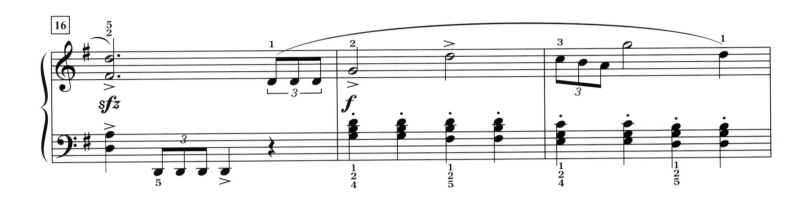

STYLE

Words and Music by Ali Payami,
Johan Schuster, Max Martin and Taylor Swift
Arr. Dan Coates

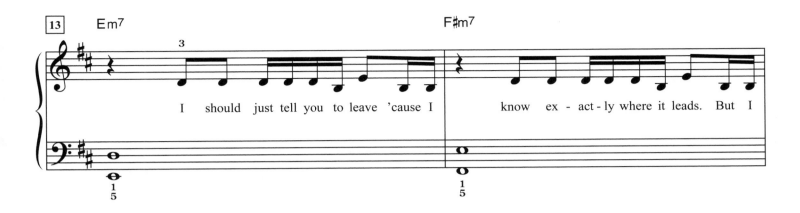

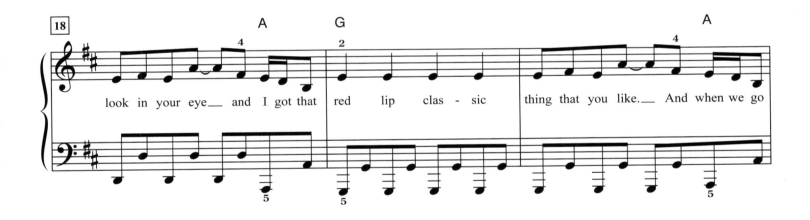

home. _____ Yeah, _____ just take me home. _____

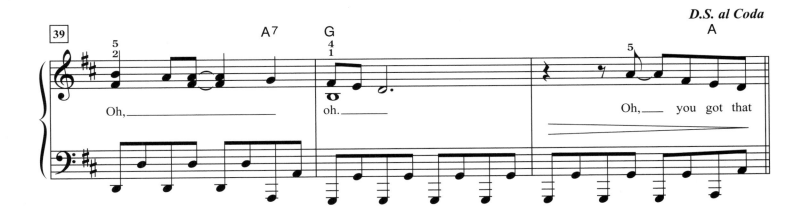

D.S. al Coda

Oh, _____ oh. _____ Oh, _____ you got that

out of style, _____ we nev-er go out of style. _____

Verse 2:
So it goes.
He can't keep his wild eyes on the road.
Take me home.
Lights are off, he's taking off his coat.
I say I heard, oh,
That you been out and about with some other girl.
He says
What you heard is true but I
Can't stop thinking 'bout you and I,
I said I've been there too a few times.
(To Chorus:)

USED TO LOVE YOU

Words and Music by Julia Cavazos, Justin Tranter,
Gwen Stefani, Teal Douville and Jonathan Rotem
Arr. Dan Coates

WANT TO WANT ME

Words and Music by Samuel Martin, Ian Kirkpatrick,
Lindy Robbins, Mitch Allan and Jason Desrouleaux
Arr. Dan Coates

WHAT DO YOU MEAN

Words and Music by Mason Levy,
Justin Bieber and Jason Boyd
Arr. Dan Coates

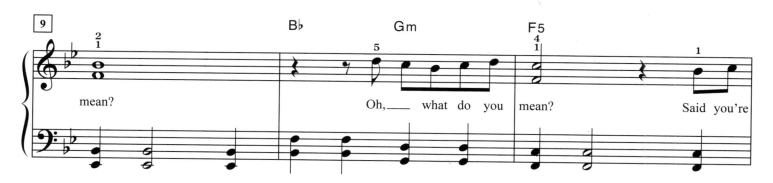

99

FLICKER

(Kanye West Rework)

Words and Music by
Mike Dean, Ella Yelich-O'Connor,
Noah Goldstein and Kanye West
Arr. Dan Coates

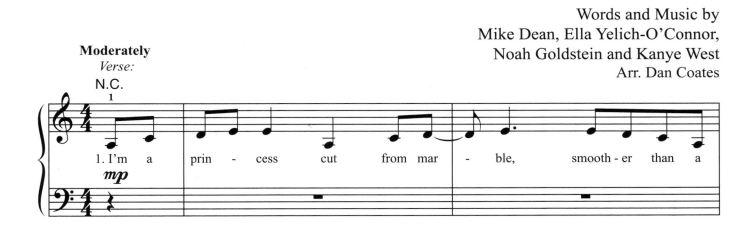

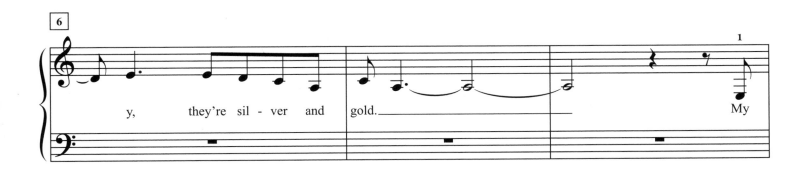